Oklahoma

OKLAHOMA

A Buddy Book
by
Julie Murray

ABDO
Publishing Company

VISIT US AT

www.abdopub.com

Published by ABDO Publishing Company, 4940 Viking Drive, Edina, Minnesota 55435.

Printed in the United States.

Edited by: Sarah Tieck
Contributing Editor: Michael P. Goecke
Graphic Design: Deb Coldiron, Maria Hosley
Image Research: Sarah Tieck
Photographs: Banana Stock, Clipart.com, Corbis, Eyewire, Getty Images, Image Ideas, Library of Congress, One Mile Up, Photodisc

Library of Congress Cataloging-in-Publication Data

Murray, Julie, 1969-
   Oklahoma / Julie Murray.
      p. cm. — (The United States)
   Includes index.
   Contents: A snapshot of Oklahoma — Where is Oklahoma? — All about Oklahoma — Cities and the capital — Famous citizens — Native Americans — The Sooner State — Tragedy in Oklahoma — A history of Oklahoma.
   ISBN 1-59197-695-2
      1. Oklahoma—Juvenile literature. I. Title.

F694.3.M87 2005
976.6—dc22

                                           2005047826

Table Of Contents

A Snapshot Of Oklahoma

Oklahoma has much history and culture. Its culture includes cowboys and Native Americans. Its landscape includes rugged mountains, grassy plains, rich farmland, and thick forests.

There are 50 states in the United States. Every state is different. Each state has an official nickname. Oklahoma is nicknamed "The Sooner State." When its land was made available to settlers in the 1880s, some people arrived "sooner" than they were supposed to and claimed land.

4

Oklahoma became the 46th state on November 16, 1907. Today, it is the 18th-largest state in America. It has 69,903 square miles (181,048 sq km) of land. It is home to 3,450,654 people.

Oklahoma City is a city in Oklahoma.

Where Is Oklahoma?

There are four parts of the United States. Each part is called a region. Each region is in a different area of the country. The United States Census Bureau says the four regions are the Northeast, the South, the Midwest, and the West.

Sometimes Oklahoma has tornadoes.

Oklahoma is located in the South region of the United States. Oklahoma has a warm, dry climate.

Four Regions of the United States of America

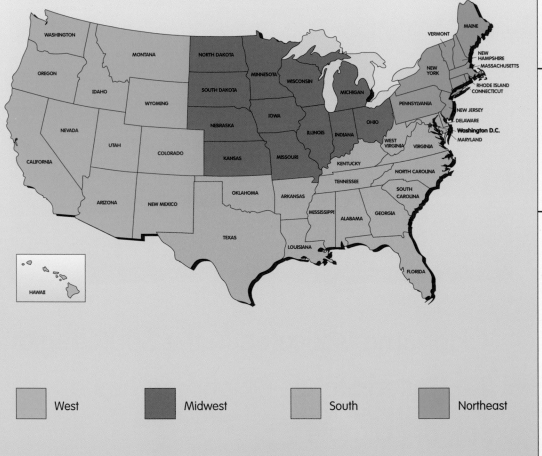

West   Midwest   South   Northeast

Oklahoma is bordered by six other states. Colorado and Kansas are found to the north. Missouri and Arkansas are east. Texas is to the south and west. The state of New Mexico is also to the west.

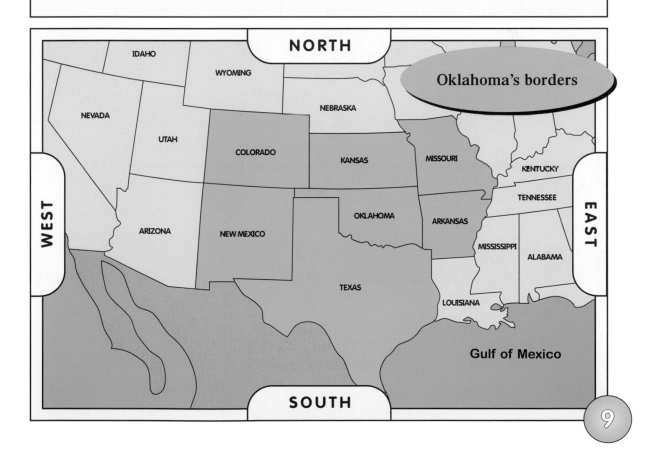

Oklahoma

State abbreviation: OK

State nickname: The Sooner State

State capital: Oklahoma City

State motto: *Labor omnia vincit* (Latin for "Labor Conquers All Things")

Statehood: November 16, 1907, 46th state

Population: 3,450,654, ranks 27th

State flag:
Adopted in 1925

OKLAHOMA

Land area: 69,903 square miles (181,048 sq km), ranks 18th

State song: "Oklahoma!"

State government: Three branches: legislative, executive, and judicial

Average July temperature: 82°F (28°C)

Average January temperature: 37°F (3°C)

State flower: Mistletoe

State bird: Scissor-tailed flycatcher

State tree: Redbud

Cities And The Capital

Oklahoma City is the capital city of Oklahoma. It is also the largest city in the state. About one-third of the state's entire population lives there. This city produces much of the oil in the United States.

Tulsa is the second-largest city in Oklahoma. It is located on the banks of the Arkansas River. It is also an important city for producing oil for the United States.

Men work with machines to produce oil in Oklahoma City.

Famous Citizens

Mickey Mantle (1931–1995)

Mickey Mantle was born in Spavinaw in 1931. From 1951 to 1968, he was a New York Yankee. Mantle was one of the greatest home run hitters in baseball history. He hit 536 home runs during his career, and had a record 18 home runs in various World Series. In 1974, Mantle was inducted into the National Baseball Hall of Fame.

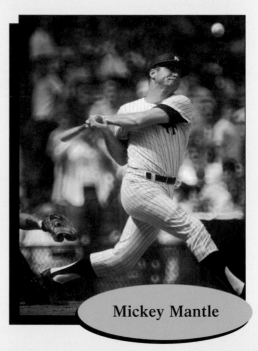

Mickey Mantle

Famous Citizens

Will Rogers (1879–1935)

Will Rogers was born near Oologah in 1879. When Rogers was born, Oklahoma was known as Indian Territory. Rogers started out as a cowboy. But he was known for many things, especially his humor. Rogers gave speeches. He wrote a newspaper column that was published in 350 papers. He was in movies and on the radio. He also wrote six books.

Will Rogers

Oklahoma's name came from the Choctaw Native Americans. *Okla* means "people" and *homma* means "red." The Native Americans have a long history in the state of Oklahoma.

Early Native American tribes lived in the grasslands. There, they hunted bison. There were several main Native American tribes that lived in Oklahoma. These were the Wichita, Comanche, Osage, Arapaho, Caddo, Pawnee, Cheyenne, and Kiowa.

A herd of bison eating grass.

Thousands of pioneers headed west in the 1800s. Back then, the western part of the United States was a great wilderness. As the United States changed, the Native Americans who lived in the southeast were forced to move. The United States Government gave them land to live on. This was called the Indian Territory. The Indian Territory included Oklahoma.

A Cheyenne
Native American

Volunteers reenact the journey Native Americans made on the Trail of Tears.

In 1838, the Cherokee Native Americans were forced to move to the Indian Territory. On the way, they faced hunger, disease, and cold weather. Thousands of Native Americans died during this trip. This is why this journey became known as the "Trail of Tears."

The Native American culture is important to Oklahoma today. More than 60 different Native American tribes live in the state. This is one of the largest Native American populations in the United States.

A Native American man dressed in traditional clothing.

The Land Run

In 1889, the United States Government opened Oklahoma to white settlers. The government purchased land from the Native American tribes. More than 3 million acres (1,214,057 ha) of land became available to the public.

At noon on April 22, a shot was fired. More than 50,000 people raced to claim land in Oklahoma. This was called the Land Run.

People raced to claim land.

Not all people played by the rules to claim their land. Some people went in early. They were called "sooners" because they went in too soon.

Today, Oklahoma's nickname is "The Sooner State." This name was inspired by the story of the Land Run.

Oil

Oil is a very important product that comes from Oklahoma. Oil is used for fuel. It helps cars run. It also helps provide power to heat houses and turn on the lights.

Oil comes from petroleum. Petroleum is pumped out of rocks in the ground.

An oil refinery in Oklahoma.

An oil well pumps oil from the ground.

Oklahoma produces much of the oil for the United States. This is why visitors to the state of Oklahoma will notice many oil wells. There is even an oil well on the grounds of Oklahoma's capitol.

Oklahoma

1541: Francisco Vasquez de Coronado explores Oklahoma.

1803: President Thomas Jefferson arranges for the United States to buy Oklahoma as part of the Louisiana Purchase.

Thomas Jefferson

1824: Fort Gibson and Fort Townsend are the first military posts in Oklahoma.

1830: Native Americans begin moving to the Indian Territory. This will later become Oklahoma.

1889: Settlers claim land in the Land Run.

1907: Oklahoma becomes the 46th state on November 16.

1970: The McClellan-Kerr Arkansas River Navigation System opens. This is used to ship products.

1995: A bomb explodes in the Alfred P. Murrah Federal Building in Oklahoma City. This destroys the building and 168 people die.

2000: Oklahoma City National Memorial opens to honor those killed in the 1995 bombing.

The Oklahoma City National Memorial

Cities In Oklahoma

Enid

Oologah Spavinaw

Tulsa

Muskogee

★ Oklahoma City

Lawton

Important Words

capital a city where government leaders meet.

Louisiana Purchase a deal where the United States bought land from France. Part of this land later became Oklahoma.

nickname a name that describes something special about a person or a place.

pioneers people who traveled across the United States in the 1800s to settle the western United States.

wilderness wild, unsettled land.

Web Sites

To learn more about Oklahoma, visit ABDO Publishing Company on the World Wide Web. Web site links about Oklahoma are featured on our Book Links page. These links are routinely monitored and updated to provide the most current information available.

www.abdopub.com

Index